Christmas in
AUSTRALIA

Christmas trees adorn many public places during the holiday season in Australia. This tree stands tall in Martin Place in Sydney.

Christmas in AUSTRALIA

Christmas Around the World
From World Book

World Book, Inc.

a Scott Fetzer company

CHICAGO   LONDON   SYDNEY   TORONTO

STAFF

President
  Robert C. Martin
Vice President and Publisher
  Michael Ross

Editorial

Managing Editor
  Maureen Mostyn Liebenson

Associate Editor
  Karen Zack Ingebretsen

Writer
  Ellen Hughes

Permissions Editor
  Janet T. Peterson

Director, Product Development
    and Research Services
  Paul Kobasa

Art

Executive Director
  Roberta Dimmer

Art Director
  Wilma Stevens

Senior Designer
  Brenda B. Tropinski

Senior Photographs Editor
  Sandra Dyrlund

Photographs Editor
  Carol Parden

For information on sales to schools and
libraries, call 1-800-975-3250.

World Book, Inc.
233 N. Michigan Ave.
Chicago, Illinois 60601
http://www.worldbook.com

Printed in Singapore
2 3 4 5 6 7 8 9 10 01 00

Product Production

Director of Manufacturing/Pre-Press
  Sandra Van den Broucke

Manufacturing/Inventory Specialist
  Mike Magusin

Senior Production Manager
  Randi Park

Production Assistant
  Linda Ebersold

Proofreaders
  Anne Dillon
  Carol Seymour

"Green Mountains" excerpt by permission
    of Envirobook, Sydney, Australia.
"Christmas in Australia" carol by permission
    of Lorna C. Parker.
  Music for "O Little Babe of Bethlehem"
    from INTERNATIONAL BOOK OF
    CHRISTMAS CAROLS. By
    permission of Walter Ehret.
    Lyrics by permission of St. Mary's
    College for the IBVM religious order.
"Tangmalangaloo" from AROUND
    THE BOREE LOG by John O'Brien
    (P.J. Hartigan). By permission of
    HarperCollins Publishers Pty. Ltd.

Library of Congress Cataloging-in-Publication Data
Christmas in Australia.
    p. cm.–(Christmas around the world from World Book)
Summary: Describes the celebration of Christmas in Australia,
including recipes, crafts projects, and elements of the indigenous
culture.
    ISBN 0-7166-0850-2
    1. Christmas—Australia—Juvenile literature. 2. Australia—Social
life and customs—Juvenile literature. [1. Christmas—Australia.
2. Australia—Social life and customs. 3. Christmas decorations.
4. Handicraft.] I. World Book Encyclopedia, Inc. II. Series.
GT4987.89.C483 1998
394.2663–dc21   98-29945

CONTENTS

The Season of Wonder in the Land
DOWN UNDER

Australia is like no other country in the world. It is the only country that is also a continent. Dazzling, world-class cities dot its coast, and the vast outback stretches inland to some of the most isolated, desolate places on earth.

Like the country itself, Christmas in Australia is like Christmas no place else. When Europeans came to live here, they brought their beliefs, customs, and attitudes of the holiday with them. And many of these traditions are still quite evident. But today there is so much more to Christmas in Australia. The holiday celebration is now a colorful blend of the customs and traditions of the many cultural groups that have come to call this exotic land "home."

The vast interior of Australia is mostly desert. The interior, known as the outback, consists mainly of open countryside, including wide expanses of grazing land.

Australia's coat of arms (below) bears many symbols of this country-continent. Australia's flag has a British Union flag, five stars for the constellation Southern Cross, and a star for the states and territories.

Port Campbell National Park in Victoria (above) is home to some of the most famous geological formations in Australia. Sheer limestone cliffs have been eaten away by the ferocious ocean, leaving behind tall pillars of more resilient rock.

The golden wattle, shown here in full bloom, is Australia's national flora emblem.

To fully appreciate how the traditions of Christmas in Australia have evolved, one must understand how this country-continent has evolved. One also must learn a bit about the geography and climate of this, the world's sixth largest country and the smallest continent in area.

Australia lies between the South Pacific and Indian oceans. It is about 7,000 miles southwest of North America and about 2,000 miles southeast of mainland Asia. It is often referred to as being "down under" because it lies entirely within the Southern Hemisphere.

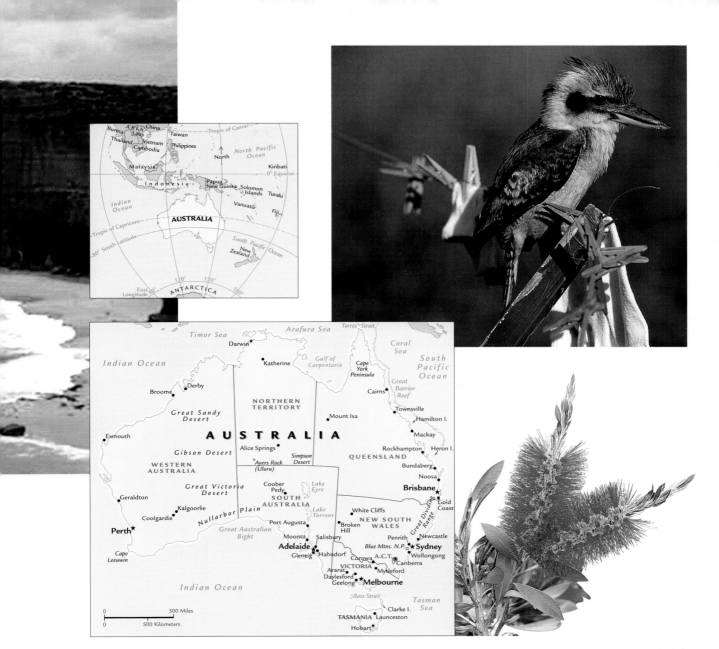

The huge interior of Australia is mostly desert or dry grassland. It is famous for its vast open spaces, bright sunshine, enormous numbers of sheep and cattle, and unusual wildlife. Kangaroos, koalas, platypuses, and wombats are only a few of the many interesting animals that live here.

Australia is comprised of six states—New South Wales, Victoria, Queensland, South Australia, Western Australia, and Tasmania—and two territories—Northern Territory and Australian Capital Territory. New South Wales is the most populous state, with 5½ million people.

Australia is surrounded by water, like an island. But because of its size, it is classified as a continent.

The kookabura bird (top) has a call that sounds like a loud laugh. Bottlebrush flowers (bottom) add color to the Australian Christmas decor.

Appreciating
Australia's Indigenous Cultures

Australia's multicultural population includes two groups of indigenous people. Aborigines, the larger and better known group, live on the mainland and the large island of Tasmania to the southeast; and Torres Strait Islanders come from the group of small islands situated off the northeastern tip of the continent. Both groups have lived in Australia for many thousands of years.

Today, indigenous Australians live in many locations. Some remain on, or have returned to, their traditional lands. Others reside in cities and towns. The lifestyles of indigenous Australians, like those of all people, have changed over time. However, many of their beliefs, as well as the structures and responsibilities of families and clan groups, continue to be very important to them.

Most indigenous Australians are Christians and celebrate Christmas in much the same way as other Christians do. This, however, has not always been the case.

Although Europeans visited Australia and observed Aborigines during the seventeenth century, these visitors did not establish settlements until 1788. They had experienced life in the cities, towns, and villages of their home countries far away, where family groups were small, governments made the laws, and religion was organized and practiced through the churches. They did not understand the richness of indigenous Australian lifestyles, or the rules for living, including family and clan relationships. Neither were Europeans aware of the belief systems of indigenous Australians.

An Aboriginal artist paints her vision of "the Dreaming." According to the Aborigines, the Dreaming was when the world was created and the relationships among all things were established by powerful gods and forces.

The Olgas are a gigantic jumble of rocks that lie 39 miles away from Ayers Rock and hide a maze of fascinating gorges and crevasses.

The world views of indigenous Australians account for the past, present, and future. They believe that they belong to the land in the same way that their families, clans, and ancestors always have. The land and all features of it—the people, mountains, rivers, seas, animals, trees, and rocks, among other things, were created by ancestor spirits. The sun, moon, constellations, winds, and rain were also created in this way. Indigenous Australian beliefs are all-encompassing—everything in the natural environment has a significant role and must be respected.

These beliefs and rules for living are expressed through the "Dreaming" stories of Aborigines and the Legends of Torres Strait Islanders. When Europeans began to "Christianize" indigenous Australians, the two sets of beliefs came together as one.

The misunderstandings of encroaching European settlers led to many violent encounters during the period of Australia's colonization. The government of Australia has recently begun a process of negotiation with indigenous people. Australians of all backgrounds hope that past differences will be reconciled, and that plans will be made for a shared future for all.

There are now efforts to display the many cultures of Australia in activities and celebrations. Australians are increasingly including Aboriginal stories, dance, music, and paintings in their Christmas experience. Cross-cultural Christmas celebrations are also presented for tourists. One such celebration takes place at Ayers Rock (known by indigenous peoples as Uluru), the magnificent rock formation in the center of the continent. Visitors spend Christmas Eve in quiet observation at this place of great Aboriginal significance, where they can enjoy a picnic meal or a toast and listen to didgeridoos as the sun sets over the rock.

The first Australians were a dark-skinned people known today as Aborigines. These people and nature shared this continent for at least 40,000 to 60,000 years—and probably even longer—before the British reached the east coast in 1788. In search of a prison colony, nearly 1,500 whites arrived on those first ships; about 750 of them were convicts. Some 300,000 Aborigines lived in Australia at the time.

Christmas in Australia is...filled with good cheer, good sporting fun, and the one-of-a-kind magic found only in this fascinating part of the world.

Until the mid-1900's, the majority of Australia's immigrants came from Britain and Ireland. As a result, most Australians are of British or Irish ancestry. But at the end of World War II, Australia began a special program to encourage mainland Europeans left homeless by the war to move to Australia. Since then, Australia has become home to about 4¾ million immigrants. Approximately half of them have come from the British Isles. Most of the rest have come from mainland Europe, especially such southern European countries as Greece and Italy. And since the 1970's, the number of immigrants from New Zealand and Southeast Asia has increased rapidly. Today, Australia boasts a population of about 18 million.

Because of Australia's rich cultural diversity, Christmas in this country is becoming a truly unique celebration with ever-evolving customs and traditions.

CHRISTMAS COMES TO AUSTRALIA

The first thing to know about Christmas in Australia is that it comes in the country's summertime, when temperatures can range from 80 °F to well over 100 °F. The next thing to know is that it is Australian—which means it is filled with good cheer, good sporting fun, and the one-of-a-kind magic found only in this fascinating part of the world.

Many of the Europeans who arrived from Britain in the late 1700's were shocked by the wildly exotic animals and plants of this vast continent. And the newcomers were over-whelmed by the land itself and its weather. To some, Christmas in the summer heat of Australia was simply bizarre.

Such thoughts are something their great-great-great-grand-children might never understand. For most Australians today, Christmas is a day to be enjoyed at the beach or at some other outdoor venue. Taking full advantage of the beauty of their natural surroundings and the warm summer days and nights, many Australians head outdoors and celebrate the holiday season.

For Australian schoolchildren, the timing of Christmas could not be better. They wrap up their studies, and then, just days before Christmas, school closes for a long summer break. Classes will not meet again until February.

School Christmas pageants, with their mix of traditional winter wonderland Christmas songs and some good hot-weather Australian carols, wrap up the school year and open the Christmas season for children.

This favorite verse of Australian children catches the spirit of the season:

Santa is known for getting a little silly in Australia.

The Twelve Days of Christmas

(last verse)

On the twelfth day of Christmas, my true love sent to me:

~ twelve koalas clowning,

~ eleven lizards leaping,

~ ten dingoes dancing,

~ nine numbats knitting,

~ eight quokkas cooking,

~ seven mice a-marching,

~ six penguins peeping,

~ five crocodiles,

~ four pelicans,

~ three lorikeets,

~ two wallabies,

~ and a bellbird in a flame tree.

Outdoor Christmas decorations are becoming more and more popular in Australian communities. This house in Queensland is an excellent example of this growing trend.

You probably recognize this carol, but you may not be familiar with some of the exotic animals used in this version. Here's a little help: a numbat is an Australian marsupial; a quokka is a small, short-tailed wallaby, which is a marsupial that is related to the kangaroo but generally smaller and with a colorful coat; a lorikeet is a brilliantly colored Australasian parrot; and a bellbird is a tropical bird that has a bell-like call.

CHRISTMAS BUSH AND CHRISTMAS LIGHTS

Most Australians trim a Christmas tree—whether real or artificial—early in December. And many decorate their homes with wattle flowers, bottle brush, and cuttings from Australia's own "Christmas bush," the *Ceratopetalum gummiferum,* a lush plant with dark green leaves and abundant red flowers that bloom just in time for the holidays.

Outdoor lights and decorations have become more and more popular around Australia, with nativity scenes and Santa and his team appearing on lawns everywhere. However, no one can hold a candle—or a string of lights—to a man named Len Doof.

Every night for three weeks during the Christmas season, Len Doof's home in the Salisbury North suburb of Adelaide (the capital of the state of South Australia) shines out its claim to being the largest private Christmas light show in the world. Doof has arranged more than 47,000 mostly hand-painted lights, controlled by 19 computers and 10⅓ miles of cable—all synchronized to Christmas music.

In Lobethal, near Adelaide, no one house stands out with a Christmas lights display. Every house does. For more than 50 years, the houses of this pretty little Adelaide Hills town have joined together to light the night at Christmastime. Each year, the displays change, but the community spirit remains the same. In the center of town, a living nativity scene—complete with cows, a donkey, and even a dove—provides a lovely focus for the twinkling lights all around. Such Christmas displays are becoming more common in other areas of Australia, as well.

WAITING FOR SANTA

On Christmas Eve, Australian children hang their stockings either on their bedposts or near a fireplace. The youngsters hold high hopes that the socks will be filled with chocolates, other candies, and little presents when Santa makes his rounds. Now and then the jolly old man squeezes his way down a chimney; but most likely he enters through a door or window.

Youngsters provide Santa with treats such as lamingtons, which are cake squares smothered in coconut.

To keep Santa energized on this first leg of his round-the-world mission, Australian youngsters leave snacks such as chocolate cake or lamingtons. Lamingtons are an Australian treat of sponge cake cubes covered in chocolate icing and dried coconut. At other times of the year, they are a popular accompaniment to afternoon tea. To drink, the children leave Santa a glass of ice-cold lemonade. The reindeer get carrots and other vegetables or grass and a bucket of cool water.

The Australian Christmas Tree

Christmas trees show up everywhere during the holiday season in Australia, even on beaches. This decorated tree stands on Bondi Beach in Sydney.

A decorated tree is essential in every town square and nearly every living room at Christmastime in Australia. Australia's only native "Christmas tree" is the radiata plantation pine. To satisfy the market for live trees, the government's forestry department grows stands of "yuletide pine," which it sells to various service clubs and charities for use in fund-raisers during the holiday season. Most who want a live tree want a pine tree. However, lately more and more families are picking up the tradition of their ancestors and using a cutting from a eucalyptus, or gum, tree to make the celebration uniquely Australian. Eucalyptus trees are the tallest trees in the country and among the tallest in the world.

For the majority of Australians, however, a bushy artificial Christmas tree, either green or metallic, makes the most sense for a summertime Christmas celebration. Trees pop up all over Australia in the first week of December, although some are not decorated until Christmas Eve, following family traditions.

Decorations for the tree range from the traditional twinkling lights, glass baubles, tinsel (as garlands are called in Australia), stars, Santas, and angels to handmade Australian ornaments fashioned from exotic seed pods, gum nuts, and berries.

Public Christmas trees are also very much a part of Christmas in Australia. Every town, park, and shopping center has a tree of its own placed in the center of the celebration. In fact, the largest Christmas tree in the Southern Hemisphere stands in the elegant Queen Victoria Shopping Center in Sydney. The massive artificial pine weighs 11,000 pounds and rises three stories to the building's famous stained-glass central dome. With 21,000 small lights, 4,000 golden balls, and 1,500 gold and green ribbons to be hung on 1,868 branches, which need placing and fluffing themselves, decorating the tree takes about a dozen people two full evenings.

In Sydney, perhaps the most famous tree is one that sings. Every December at the Grace Brothers department store, more than 20 choristers stand in a steel tree-shaped structure to entertain shoppers on their missions for Santa.

In Exmouth, an isolated town on the coast of northern Western Australia situated many miles from the nearest pine tree, residents look forward each year to the Festival of Trees. Here, local businesses present the town with a hall full of sparkling artificial trees, each decorated to reflect its patron's line of work. Businesses in Adelaide follow suit, sponsoring trees set in forestlike clusters in the city's Rundle Mall. Here, the trees are dressed by specially chosen celebrity decorators.

A "tree" made up of wreaths of graduated sizes towers over shoppers in this Sydney mall.

Waking on Christmas morning, children dive right into their stockings filled with treats. But they must wait for Mum and Dad to get up before checking out the presents under the tree. Once the gifts are unwrapped, many families head to an outdoor celebration, to Pop and Nana's, or to an uncle and auntie's home for more presents and Christmas dinner with the whole family.

CHRISTMAS AT THE BEACH

More than 70 percent of the population of Australia resides in one of the six state capitals that hug the coasts of Australia—Sydney, New South Wales; Melbourne, Victoria; Brisbane, Queensland; Perth, Western Australia; Adelaide, South Australia; and Hobart, Tasmania. Although most of the people who live in these cities work in modern steel-and-glass structures, even the most urban find themselves in close company with nature. A multitude of magnificent beaches and parks is within easy reach. It is no surprise, then, that in addition to the backyard poolside barbecue, the beach is a popular destination for Christmas dinner.

In Melbourne, Brighton Beach has always been a premiere spot to celebrate Christmas. In Sydney, Bondi Beach is a favorite. A good thing about the beach is that there is room for everyone and for every kind of celebration. Beachside cafes, food stands, and shops can supply anything forgotten at home and plenty that looks too good to pass up. There is

Even the most urban find themselves in close company with nature.

music everywhere and plenty of pick-up games of soccer and volleyball. And where else can revelers enjoy a refreshing splash in the water after dinner or between bites? Even the seaside police get in the mood, wearing elves' caps as they bike along the walkways. At Bondi Beach, things heat up even more on New Year's Eve, with live entertainment, street performers, amusement rides, and fireworks.

ISLAND CHRISTMAS

In Sydney, ocean-loving picnickers can reserve a private picnic spot on one of the tiny islands of Sydney Harbour. Protect-
ed from development, the islands remain little bits of wilder-
ness in the middle of the busy port. Permission to visit an island must be obtained in advance, so those making Christmas
picnic plans can be assured of privacy on their day.

Picnic island choices include Shark Island, with a lovely
pavilion and grottos; tiny Clarke Island, which can take only 15
picnic-goers at a time and Spectacle Island, which was the site
of the country's first Royal Naval Base.

Nearby marine services ferry celebrants to and from the islands and can even supply gourmet barbecues and picnics for
those giving the gift of an island for Christmas.

*As temperatures soar, many
Australians head outdoors to
celebrate the holiday season.
Here, coworkers enjoy a
Christmas picnic lunch in
Melbourne.*

From Perth to Brisbane, and Darwin to Hobart, Australians observe the holiday at church services.

CAROLS AT CHURCH

Whether on Christmas Eve, Christmas Day, or both, Australians attend Christmas church services in record numbers. Carol-singing is at the heart of the religious celebration here, and cathedrals in the major cities offer some spectacular performances.

Two cathedrals that draw tremendous crowds for midnight Mass are St. Mary's cathedral in Sydney and St. Patrick's cathedral in Melbourne. And St. Paul's cathedral in Melbourne offers both a midnight Mass with a visiting choir and string quartet and a Christmas morning choral service.

In Adelaide, St. Peter's begins with a children's service late in the afternoon on Christmas Eve. Children take part in the blessing of the Nativity scene and in decorating the Christmas tree. As the evening begins, the rest of the church congregation is welcome to join in a carol procession.

THE CHRISTMAS FEAST

Starting when Australia opened its doors to immigrants after World War II, the Christmas menu has experienced a gradual change. Today, 4 out of every 10 Australians are first- or second-generation immigrants, and half of them come from non-English-speaking backgrounds. This cultural diversity adds a delicious difference to modern Australian Christmas fare. Greek, Italian, and Asian immigrants especially have made their mark on Australian cuisine by adding new tastes. And popular restaurants feature Lebanese, Turkish, Balkan, Hungarian, and Spanish dishes.

More surprising—and delightful—Christmas fare is coming from Australians' new appreciation of "home-grown" Australian food. "Bush tucker," or, when served in gourmet restaurants, "native cuisine," is all the rage in Australia today. The emergence of this Australian culinary tradition is part of a growing nationalism, in which Australia can be seen moving away from Great Britain and forging an identity of its own.

Prepared in updated recipes and served with a mixture of traditional British and Asian fare, such Australian offerings as possum, crocodile, kangaroo, and emu are turning up on the table.

Surprising—and delightful—Christmas fare is coming from Australians' new appreciation of "home-grown" Australian food.

Add to that Australia's vast storehouse of tasty berries, nuts, and herbs, and you have the makings of a unique holiday feast.

But while this native cuisine is gaining in popularity, many Australians still serve the traditional turkey for Christmas dinner.

Australians enjoy the British tradition of snapping Christmas crackers on Christmas Day. These colorfully wrapped paper tubes make a popping sound when opened.

However, they are not likely to eat it sitting around the dining room table in their fanciest clothing. Often, the turkey is served cold as part of a buffet luncheon to be enjoyed in the shade of the yard, by the pool, in the park, or at the beach.

And the turkey usually has plenty of company. The main course is likely to be accompanied by a selection of cold ham, chicken, duck, and other meats, plus squid, oysters, salmon, prawns, and other fresh seafood ready to grill. There often is an array of vegetables and salad offerings, and the buffet table may be stocked with apricots, peaches, plums, bananas, grapes, mangos, and melons of every color, plus bowls of berries and cherries.

Suiting the heat of the season and the spirit of celebration, the meal is usually offered with plenty of Australian champagne, wine, and beer. The children quench their thirst with lemonade and soft drinks.

Either placed beside each plate or packed in the picnic hamper are likely to be Christmas crackers, also called poppers or bon bons. A British tradition that has found a permanent home in Australia, these brightly wrapped paper tubes are tied at each end. They are called crackers because of the noise they make when popped open. They usually contain a trinket or two, a colorful paper party hat, and a corny riddle for the children to read aloud.

Another British Christmas tradition that lives on in the hearts and stomachs of many Australians is plum pudding. In their light-hearted fashion, some Australians are pretty serious about their plum pudding. In 1987, employees of Herbert Adams's store in Kensington, Victoria, set a record by cooking the world's largest Christmas pudding—a whopper that weighed in at just over 3,000 pounds.

Another famous plum pudding is "Father Mac's Heavenly

Pudding." In 1985, needing funds to fix up a rundown church in northern New South Wales, Father Darcy McCarthy turned to his mother's old recipes and began baking cakes and Christmas puddings to sell at church events.

Father Mac's puddings were especially wonderful, and soon orders were coming by phone and by mail from all over Australia, as well as overseas. In 1987, the good Father—and good cook—prepared 11,000 puddings himself, setting his alarm to wake him every two hours around the clock so he could rise and start another batch.

By 1991, Father Mac and his helpers were producing 50,000 puddings for Christmas. Today, four staff members and 25 volunteers continue cooking for a good cause. The church group sends out more than 560,000 "puds" each year in two sizes—28 ounces and 3½ pounds.

The success of Father Mac's endeavor is proof that many Australians are not interested in putting in the hot hours in the kitchen that "homemade" plum pudding requires. But no matter who makes the pudding, it always has pressed into it coins or other small trinkets to be discovered by lucky diners. Various trinkets symbolize good luck, health, or marriage in the coming year to some families. To others, the trinkets are just the means for a fun "treasure hunt."

Today other treats join plum pudding on the Australian Christmas dessert table. One is pavlova, a large, circular meringue shell filled with fresh whipped cream and fruit.

What's the Word?

barbie . . . . barbeque

chook . . . . chicken

kip . . . . sleep

ripper . . . . terrific

tucker . . . . food

While Australians celebrate Christmas in their own unique style, it seems their traditions will continue to evolve. After more than 200 years, the people of this exotic land are beginning to truly appreciate their ancestry, their history, and the products native to their land.

Christmas Cheer and
CELEBRATION

The "Run-Up to Christmas," as the weeks and days just before Christmas are called in Australia, is filled with parades, festivals, carol-singing, and celebration. Taking full advantage of their warm summer weather, Australians celebrate in the great outdoors and share the fun all around.

More than 100,000 people line the streets of downtown Adelaide to watch the Credit Union Christmas Pageant. This annual parade ushers Santa Claus into the city to officially begin the Christmas season.

CHRISTMAS ON PARADE

The biggest and most brilliant pageant, or parade, of all is the beloved Credit Union Christmas Pageant, which brings the city of Adelaide to a merry stop and opens the city's Christmas season each year. Onlookers line the streets along the two-mile parade route in downtown Adelaide to greet Santa as he makes his arrival to the city.

Until a few years ago, this popular parade was called John Martin's Christmas Pageant, as it was sponsored by John Martin's Department Store. However, the department store met with financial hardship and was bought out by another store. The government of Adelaide decided that the parade was too special to risk losing it. So today it is sponsored by the Events Council of the city government and by the Credit Union.

What is now an annual tradition began as a notion of John Martin's Department Store owner Sir Edward Hayward, who was looking for a way to raise people's spirits during the Great Depression. To attract attention for his first pageant in 1933, Hayward hired two Tiger Moth airplanes and instructed the pilots to fly over the suburbs, announcing "Father Christmas is coming this morning!" over loudspeakers. Trams were packed and train stations crowded as 100,000 people rushed to the city's center to watch floats, bands, and Santa Claus himself parade through Adelaide.

Costumed characters, including this happy clown, help provide the entertainment for Adelaide's Credit Union Christmas Pageant.

Today, the parade continues to bring Santa to town at the start of every holiday season. These days, the jolly old fellow finds himself at the end of a parade procession that also includes over 900 costumed characters, more than 50 dazzling floats of fantasy, and as many as a dozen bands.

Other cities around the world may have longer parade processions, but no spectators turn out to cheer like the citizens of Adelaide. It is estimated that one-third of the city's residents, or about 350,000 people, are joined by tourists to make a total crowd of 500,000. At the end of the two-hour parade, any and all are welcome to a citywide picnic at Elder Park.

Across the continent in Perth, the capital and business center of Western Australia, Santa comes to town in that city's Christmas Pageant. This parade, sponsored by a local television station, is a child's wonderland of brilliantly lighted floats, fairy lights, tumbling clowns, and dancers. More than 400,000 spectators come to take in the sights and sounds of this holiday procession.

Starting at the city's center, the pageant's 2,000 participants, most of whom are children, proceed to the Esplanade, a park overlooking the ocean. Cyclists, clowns, inline skaters, and dancers swirl around dazzling floats illuminated by more than 30,000 lights. The overall effect is that of a magical fairyland, a sight to spark any child's imagination.

Santa arrives in style in the little town of Broken Hill as well. Residents of this historic outback mining community flock to the

Spectators young and old enjoy what they see at the Credit Union Christmas Pageant.

The windows of Myers Department Store in Melbourne display an Australian Christmas, complete with kangaroos and koalas.

main street to cheer enthusiastically for more than 50 floats. Townspeople and schoolchildren dressed as Nativity scene figures, snowmen, and elves parade by and wave to onlookers. At last, there is Santa. And what a sport he is, dressed in full suit and beard, despite the heat that usually reaches more than 80 °F and often soars to over 100 °F.

With country music and line dancing at one point and the Cameron Pipe Band farther on, the parade makes its way to Sturt Park. Here everyone celebrates together under the rays of the summer sun while enjoying the selection of food from stalls and barbecues that line the park.

A MELBOURNE CHRISTMAS

Melbourne residents are encouraged to sing along on the Saturday before Christmas, when more than 1,000 choristers approach the city's Swanson Street Walk from different directions. Filling the streets with candlelight and song, the carolers follow people dressed as the Three Wise Men on camels to City Square. Here gifts of food for the needy are placed under Melbourne's giant Christmas tree.

On Christmas Day in Melbourne, a city famous for its charming trams, visitors can partake in a special traveling holiday treat. The city's oldest tram, and the world's only tramcar restaurant, invites passengers aboard its elegant dining car to ride through the boulevards of Melbourne. As they travel, the passengers enjoy a five-course Christmas luncheon complete with fine Australian wines and all the trimmings while taking in all the sights of Christmas. The tram departs from the National Gallery at midday to take a rambling tour of the city's leafy boulevards and gardens.

A TRIP ON A CAROL TRAIN

What fun it is to ride and sing! Especially if you are riding on the Puffing Billy Carol Train.

Every year at Christmastime, the historic Puffing Billy Railway steams away from its home station at Belgrade in the Dandenong Ranges, 25 miles from Melbourne. Carrying a full load of holiday celebrants for a caroling ride, the train chugs through the mountain scenery. At the end of the line riders enjoy a lakeside park celebration.

The Puffing Billy is the last remaining steam train to run regularly in the region of mountains and lakes that such trains helped settle in the early 1900's. Now a living-museum train, the Puffing Billy operates solely through the dedicated effort of volunteers. At Christmas, those volunteers shine up the antique train, stoke up a full head of steam, and ready plenty of holiday cheer for one extra-special trip to benefit a good cause. A joint venture of the Puffing Billy Railway and the Soroptimist International Society, the Puffing Billy Christmas Festival donates all its proceeds to the William Angliss Hospital, which has served the area since 1939.

The Puffing Billy Carol Train provides a unique ride through the hills around Belgrave. The train passes some of the most majestic forest and mountain scenery in Victoria.

The adventure starts on a balmy Saturday evening the week before Christmas at the train's Belgrade station. Here, a Christmas choir sends the crowd of festive travelers on its way. People buy sausages, juices, and snacks, making last-minute additions to their packed picnic hampers. At stops along the route, the train is greeted by local bands and singers in full holiday voice.

When the Puffing Billy arrives at Emerald Lake Park, the travelers disembark to join the hundreds of others who have come by car, bus, and bike to share in a carols-by-candlelight celebration. Local groups set up booths to offer great food, Christmas goodies, and decorations to add to the cheer and raise money for the benefit.

As the sun sets, candles are lit throughout the park, making the lake and hills appear magical. Before heading back by train, everyone enjoys an evening of picnicking and caroling under the stars.

QUEENSLAND'S CHRISTMAS LANTERN FESTIVAL

For Christmas magic, music, and all-around holiday fun, Queensland families head for the annual Christmas Lantern Festival at South Bank Parklands. Here they enjoy concerts, dances, plays, parades, even nightly fireworks. The festival brings out all the sparkle of the season during the week before Christmas Eve.

Central to this celebration is the Christmas Lantern parade. Each night during the week-long festival, beautifully designed lighted lanterns display Christmas images ranging from the Three Wise Men and the Holy Family to Santa Claus, Rudolph, and the elves. The lanterns are carried through the streets, surrounded by thousands of twinkling Christmas lights, musicians, singers, dancers, stilt walkers, and more.

Most entrancing are the celestial-themed lanterns, designed with stars, the moon, and the planets. Then there are the "star-catching" elves, who have aluminum pipes built into their costumes to produce magical percussive music reminiscent of wind chimes in the breeze. Celestial-themed lanterns also line the parkland's central walkways.

Santa, along with Rudolph and a friendly band of musicians and helpers, cruises the parkland's waterways on his own ferry.

On each night of the festival, children are welcome to step into an interactive "First Christmas" Nativity scene. In the "stable" the youngsters receive a hands-on understanding of that Christmas long ago as they talk with the actors and pet the barn animals.

The festival's Christmas tree also comes to life as the Queensland Children's Choir "takes a bough," performing on special risers that form the shape of a Christmas tree. Festival visitors are welcome to raise their voices in song during a nightly carol sing-along to the music of the Queensland Pops Orchestra and local church choirs.

On one special night during the festival, attendees are treated to "The Night the River Sings." On this night, a fleet of more than 50 spectacularly decorated and lighted private and commercial vessels cruises the Brisbane River along the parkland's edge. The boats compete for prizes in categories such as best fleet and brightest boat.

In addition, the festival offers humorous Christmas plays, roving musicians and jesters, rides, and craft fair offerings. Even Santa, along with Rudolph and a friendly band of musicians and helpers, cruises the parkland's waterways on his own ferry, waving to children and entertaining the crowds. And each night, fireworks over the water top the festival.

Queensland's Christmas Lantern Festival at South Bank Parklands offers a variety of Christmas entertainment, including parades and fireworks.

ST. NICHOLAS NIGHT IN HAHNDORF

In 1838, fifty-two German Lutheran families brought their hopes, dreams, and Christmas customs to South Australia, founding the little town of Hahndorf in the Adelaide Hills. Today, Hahndorf's German culture and food, historic churches, antique clock museum, model train winding through a miniature Bavarian village, little shops, and homemade goods draw visitors all year long. But at Christmas, with the holiday traditions of Hahndorf's founders on display, the little town is at its charming best.

On the eve of St. Nicholas Day, December 6, Santa Claus in the guise of St. Nicholas makes his annual entrance in a candle-light parade through the streets of Hahndorf. Following local custom, the bearded bishop is accompanied by two traditional "Black Peters," small, pesky servants who assist in handing out sweets to children along the route.

Townspeople join the parade, following St. Nicholas to a candlelight caroling service. Then more treats are in store, as the kindly bishop passes out tasty gingerbread men in celebration of his day.

DARLING HARBOUR'S 12 DAYS OF CHRISTMAS

In Sydney, people dressed as Mary, Joseph, and Baby Jesus lead a parade to open the annual Darling Harbour 12 Days of Christmas celebration on December 12. The Christmas cast has grown since early times. Sydney's presentation includes a symphony orchestra, more than 1,000 performers, and dozens of animals.

Given the Australian summer heat, maybe the craziest thing Santa does is stick to his traditional red suit.

If you are in Sydney during the holiday season, you are bound to find yourself at Darling Harbour again and again, for the December 12 extravaganza is only the beginning of great things to come each day leading up to Christmas Eve. Performers include acrobats, jazz musicians, barbershop quartet singers, actors, Christmas carolers, and rock-and-roll musicians.

Until the mid-1980's, this horseshoe-shaped bay on the west-

Foregoing the sleigh and reindeer, Santa Claus is rowed ashore by lifeguards on Christmas Day.

ern edge of the city's center was a wasteland of rocks and railroad yards. The whole area was redeveloped and opened in time for Australia's bicentennial in 1988. The Harbour is surrounded with shops, entertainment centers, and restaurants, all of which cater to shoppers around Christmas. From here, families can hop a ferry or charter a cruise around Sydney's spectacular chain of harbors.

SUFFERIN' SANTAS

Santa has been known to get a little silly during his Australian stopover. On Christmas Day at Heron Island on the Great Barrier Reef, Santa comes roaring up in a speedboat behind some flipper-footed "reindeer." On beaches elsewhere, he's been sighted on a surfboard. One popular Australian Christmas song puts six white boomers, or large kangaroos, pulling Santa's sleigh, although no witnesses have ever come forward.

Given the Australian summer heat, maybe the craziest thing Santa does is stick to his traditional red suit. Some have suggested that Santa follow local custom and don shorts, a singlet (a tank-top shirt), thongs, and an akubra hat when he's down under. But Santa is a stickler for tradition. Even in the scorching desert of the outback, the jolly old and very hot fellow wearing his traditional attire has visited with children. Santa does have some sense, however. While in Australia he usually opts for red cotton, skips the thick fur trim, and puts a nix on any extra padding.

CAROLS BY CANDLELIGHT

Each year, as they stand in their own distant corner of the world with the vast expanse of the rugged outback behind them, thousands of miles of ocean all around, and the Southern Cross sparkling above, thousands of Australians across the country's coast hold up candles to the warm Christmas night and sing.

"Carols by Candlelight," as this special form of celebration is known here, is at the very heart of the season in Australia. To many, it just would not be Christmas without that one night when crowds of neighbors, friends, and strangers gather to raise their voices, sending the sounds of Christmas up to the heavens.

Although today's carolers may not guess it, their caroling tradition has deep roots in Australia's past. Carols by Candlelight is generally said to have started in Melbourne in 1937. However, one account tells of Cornish miners in Moonta, South Australia, sticking "fatjacks," or tallow candles, on the front of their safety hats with a dab of damp clay to light the night when they caroled in 1865.

The miners were immigrants from Cornwall who brought with them a great love for hearty "curl" singing. These men first gathered together to sing on the mine's loading platforms toward the end of their Christmas Eve shift. On Christmas Day, they sang in church; then they caroled at homes, in hotel bars, and on street corners. Parties of young miners roved from cottage to cottage where they were welcomed, treated to homebrew, and encouraged to keep singing well into the night.

Later, Moonta's carol-singing was formalized into concerts on Christmas night in Victoria Park. Chinese lanterns hung in the trees, casting a glow on the big crowds gathered to listen to choirs from the district and join in the singing.

Carols by Candlelight is Australian in its appeal. In this country, nature is close to the heart and close at hand. From Sydney with its 70 beaches; to Melbourne, where one-third of the city is designated parkland; to the outback, where the weather is a constant force to be reckoned with, the Christmas celebration, to be meaningful, must take place, at least in part, in the great outdoors.

And to the Australians, who have always welcomed strangers to their shores and to their homes and who know the importance of a helping hand, it just wouldn't be Christmas if not everyone was invited to sing.

A large crowd gathers with candles in hand for a Carols by Candlelight celebration in Sydney (top). Children are careful with their candles at a Carols by Candlelight celebration in Melbourne (bottom).

The grandest Carols by Candlelight event of them all is Sydney's Carols in the Domain. The Domain, a breathtaking natural amphitheater in the Royal Botanic Gardens, is a splendid place to carol. Now with more than 100,000 participants, this carol-sing grows in size and significance every year.

The evening's celebration features performances by world-class musicians, including the Sydney Philharmonic Choir, Sydney Youth Orchestra, and popular musical acts, in addition to the group sing. Carols in the Domain is televised throughout Australia, New Zealand, and Southeast Asia. The Salvation Army benefits from the sale of candles at the event.

Other communities throughout Australia also take advantage of the spectacular beauty of their surroundings by staging their own Carols by Candlelight events.

The Olsens Capricorn Caves Carols by Candlelight service is one of the oldest and boasts what may be the most dramatic setting. Olsens Capricorn Caves are a series of 16 above-ground caves formed from an ancient coral reef some 380 million years ago near Rockhampton in Queensland. Today the caves are used for various parties and other events and have been the site for a carol service every Christmas for more than 110 years. The remarkable acoustics of the cavern affect the sound of the singing in a way that is described as both "electrifying" and "emotional."

Carols at the Cove, presented near Sanctuary Cove in Queensland, is an evening of family caroling set against the Cove's waterfront Marine Village.

To the Australians, who have always welcomed strangers to their shores, it just wouldn't be Christmas if not everyone was invited to sing.

In the city of Glenelg in South Australia, a heart-warming Carols by Candlelight community sing is led by the children of local schools and choir groups. There also are Carols by Candlelight celebrations in Cairns, in Darwin, at Noosa, and even on Hamilton Island on the Great Barrier Reef.

Yulefest: Christmas in July

Those who feel Christmas just isn't Christmas without cold weather can join the folks in the charming resort towns of Australia's Blue Mountains. Here they celebrate "Yulefest," complete with a traditional hot turkey dinner and all the trimmings, cozy nights by the fire, carols, and gifts. It just happens that all this takes place in July, when the weather of an Australian winter gives a frosty edge to the mountain air.

Yulefest was started by Irish tourists staying at the Mountain Heritage Retreat guesthouse. When they noticed that the July weather in the popular resort area 30 miles west of Sydney felt like Christmastime back home, they made a special request for a fitting Christmas meal. And it's been Christmas each weekend in July ever since—and in June and August, too. The decorations are on display in the towns, and you are likely to see Santa Claus strolling about.

Caught up in the Christmas spirit, various Blue Mountain resorts plan their own special Yulefest celebrations. There are caroling parties, theatrical Christmas productions, holiday games, and even presents under Christmas trees.

Of course, the December version of Christmas also is celebrated in the Blue

Santa Claus, in his traditional red garb, celebrates Christmas in July by taking to the slopes.

Mountains, which separate the cities of the coast from the country's flat, rugged interior. Here revelers can enjoy a traditional high tea by the fireside at a charming bed and breakfast and visit the tiny resort towns' cozy restaurants and unusual shops, which offer Christmas items all year long. Many city dwellers come simply to escape the summer heat they left below. They may take a stroll on the cool mountain trails, enjoy a picnic, or set up camp to vacation in the great outdoors.

The streets of downtown Sydney are aglow with Christmas lights and decorations.

Rivaling Carols in the Domain in stature is Melbourne's Carols by Candlelight at the Sydney Myer Music Bowl. The modern tradition of candlelight singing began here in 1937 and, each year, more than 30,000 people gather to keep it going strong. Special guests at the celebration include well-known musicians as well as Santa and the popular children's television character Humphrey Bear. Proceeds from the Melbourne event benefit the Royal Victorian Institute for the Blind.

Humphrey Bear also puts in an appearance at St. David's Park in Hobart, Tasmania, for that city's candlelight caroling event. Here, more than 15,000 people are expected to bring candles and sing as others have done at this event for the last 50 years.

In Adelaide, Carols by Candlelight in Elder Park presents a lineup of popular entertainers and is capped off by a fireworks display.

Live camels join the elaborate Nativity scene presented in Perth, Western Australia, during their Carols by Candlelight celebration. Participants get to see themselves as "part of the largest massed choir in the state" as they sing to the accompaniment of a full orchestra.

The historic Lanyon Homestead outside Australia's capital city of Canberra is itself lit by candlelight during its Carols by Candlelight event. Here, participants are invited to bring a picnic dinner and may even win first prize for the most colorful picnic setting.

THE GIVING SEASON

Many Australians open their hearts and their wallets to poor families at Christmastime to help spread the cheer and celebration of the season. And it's a good thing, for as many as 900,000 families in Australia can be classified as poor. In fact, Australia had one of the highest rates of child poverty in the industrialized world in 1996. And here, as in many places around the world, Christmas and the months surrounding the holiday are peak periods of demand for charities. Many families who struggle to make ends meet throughout the year can feel overwhelmed at Christmastime. It is just too hard for families with children to watch their youngsters go without at this time of year. Instead of being a joyous occasion, Christmas becomes a crisis for such families. Fortunately, Christmas is also the time of year when Australian charities receive the most donations.

In St. Kilda, a cosmopolitan bayside suburb of Melbourne, the Sacred Heart Mission has an enthusiastic team of volunteers ready to spread some Christmas cheer. The team prepares a modest feast each year for hundreds of less-fortunate families likely to join them for Christmas lunch. The destitute, the desperate, and the lonely come to the mission to partake in a little Christmas celebration.

The Exodus Foundation, an arm of the Ashfield Uniting Church of Sydney, also puts on an annual lunch on Christmas Day. The holiday meal often brings as many as 2,000 guests.

What's the Word?

arvo . . . . afternoon

cobber . . . . friend

lob . . . . arrive

mate . . . . a good friend

she's sweet . . . . everything will be all right

Australia's Christmas
PAST

The first British ships that sailed into Australia's harbors in the late 1770's brought this continent's first white inhabitants. History notes that as the first British ships sailed into Sydney's harbor, two Aborigines stood on the bank shouting "Warra! Warra!" ("Away! Away!") and vigorously waving the intruders off. But the British and their way of life—including their Christmas customs—had come to stay in Australia. Although the first Christmases in the new homeland were not always the merriest, they were still very important observances of the birth of Jesus Christ.

This engraving shows early immigrants celebrating Christmas in their new homeland. The Australian heat at Christmastime and the unique wildlife were just a
few of the many changes these settlers had to endure.

British immigrants and Australian aborigines pose together in what is believed to be the earliest photograph taken in Australia.

Most of the early British immigrants had come to their new homeland unhappily, not that it was much consolation to the Aborigines. It took a long time for many of them to see this exotic land of great beauty and amazing animals as anything other than *not* Great Britain. Life down under seemed only life far away from back home and from life as it *should* be.

At Christmas, the pull of home was strongest, making Australia's December summer sunshine, sparkling blue waters and skies, and abundance of fresh fruits and vegetables simply wrong.

The first recorded Australian Christmas service was performed by a Reverend Johnson at Sydney Cove in 1788. For Governor Arthur Phillips and his officers, a holiday meal and Christmas toast is described. For the unfortunate convicts in their charge, no plum pudding or mulled cider, but the usual bread rations. One Michael Dennison received a present of sorts. It being Christmas Day, Dennison's scheduled sentence of 200 lashes was reduced to 150.

Writing home, John Hood, a Scottish visitor to Australia in 1841, voiced a common Christmas complaint, "The sultry heat is a disagreeable contradiction to all our impressions of that happy season of frosts and snows and fireside comforts."

In Sydney or Melbourne, where summer temperatures might rise to nearly 90 °F, British wives and daughters labored in blazing hot kitchens to produce the traditional full-course Christmas dinner, from the roasted turkey with all the trimmings to the flaming plum pudding. Then, the whole family—dressed in their holiday finery—felt obliged to sit in the stuffy dining room, waving away flies and struggling through the heavy meal.

Sitting around after dinner, there was plenty of time to reconsider whether a grand piping-hot British feast was really the merriest way to celebrate Christmas in the heat of summer on the opposite side of the world.

AUSTRALIAN TRADITIONS ARE BORN

The turkey and plum pudding did seem essential year after year, but soon they were served with fresh fruits and cool drinks. Hot kitchens were left behind as families took their meals to the park or beach where they could enjoy the natural wonder of Christmas in their new-found homeland. By the late 1800's, Christmas had become the very joyful, very Australian celebration it is today.

A writer in the *Illustrated Sydney News* of 1890 took it upon himself to notify Great Britain of an Australian change of holiday plans:

"We are neither disloyal nor ungrateful, but we take leave to say that by long custom we care not for our Christmas in a bearskin. We are lovers of whatever is warm and ardent, and are not overmuch given to taking our pleasures indoors. We may still, like our English forefathers, take our pleasures rather sadly, but we like them hot.

"Therefore we tickle grim Father Christmas under his frostbitten nose with a sprig of wattle bloom . . . .

This photograph, taken around 1925, shows Father Christmas and two young friends standing in front of a giant model of a plum pudding.

The beach has been a "hot" spot for celebrating Christmas in Australia for many years, as demonstrated in this photograph from 1929.

The journalist continues:

"The season, as everybody knows, really begins on Christmas Eve. It is then that hampers are packed, all necessaries purchased, admonitions given, weak ones cautioned, and the final touches imparted to the arrangements for spending the great day itself. These things done, the world puts its hands into its pockets, smiles all round, and then retires to rest."

And Henry Lawson in his book, *Ghosts of Many Christmases*, describes a Sydney harbor Christmas scene of the late 1800's:

"Buses, electric, cable, and the old steam trams crowded with holiday-makers with baskets. Harbour boats loaded down to the water's edge with picnic-parties. Strings of tourist trains running over the Blue Mountains and the Great Zigzag, and up the coast to Gosford and Brisbane Water, and down the south coast to beautiful Illawarra.

"Jolly camps and holiday parties all round the beautiful bays of the harbour, and up and down the coast, and all close to home. Camps in the moonlight on sandy beaches under great dark bluffs and headlands, where shelving, sandstone cliffs run, broken only by sandy-beached bays, and where the silver-white breakers leap and roar."

Strolling on Melbourne's Brighton Beach, a reporter for the *Illustrated Melbourne Post* in 1864 records a similar scene:

"An impromptu encampment springs up among the tea-tree scrub which flourishes upon the sand hummocks. Fires are lit; hampers of provisions unpacked; table-cloths are spread upon the sand; temporary awnings rigged overhead; and innumerable gipsy parties, in close proximity to each other, apply themselves with British vigour to diminish the stock of comestibles and drinkables they have brought with them. The clatter of plates, the popping of corks, the jingling of glasses, and the rattle of knives and forks, mingle with peals of merry laughter, with the buzz of conversation, and the splash of the waves upon the beach."

A GOLD DIGGER'S CHRISTMAS

While civilized society toasted Christmas in style on the beaches and grassy lawns of Australia's coastal cities, the thousands of men in the bush who had poured into the country during the gold rush periods of the 1800's did their best to celebrate the season no matter where they found themselves.

Life was rough on the goldfields, from the east in the 1850's to the Kalgoorlie-Coolgardie field in western Australia in the 1890's. Striking it rich was the dream but almost never the reality. Competition

What's the Word?

billy . . . . can for boiling tea water

dinky di . . . . genuine

new chum . . . . . new migrant

O.S. . . . . overseas

was fierce. Those who did find gold ran a high risk of losing their lives to the likes of bushrangers (highwaymen) and claim-jumpers.

Diggers lived wretched lives, risking it all for the chance at riches. Home to a digger might be nothing more than a lean-to or temporary hut barely big enough to crawl into after an exhausting day. At Christmas, the privations of their lives, especially the long distance from wives, children, and friends, was hard to bear. To ease their sorrow, many diggers took it upon themselves to spread Christmas cheer.

In this 1898 account, gold digger David W. Carnegie describes his Christmas in a goldfield camp:

> "Sheltered from the sun's burning rays by our house, so low that it could only be entered on hands and knees, for we had neither time nor strength to build a spacious structure, we did our best to spend a 'Happy Christmas.'

> "Somehow, the climate and surroundings seemed singularly inappropriate; dust could not be transformed, even in imagination, into snow, nor heat into frost, any more easily than we could turn dried apples into roast beef and plum pudding . . . .

> "Having spread the table—that is, swept the floor clear of ants and other homely insects—and laid out the feast, I rose to my knees and proposed the health of my old friend and comrade Mr. Davies, wished him the compliments of the season, and expressed a hope that we should never spend a worse Christmas."

Children who encountered diggers on the street often arrived home with all the treasures they could carry.

Even in the rough and dangerous gold-rush boom towns, many lonely prospectors were known to show a soft heart at Christmastime. Diggers would round up groups of children and escort them into shops to choose Christmas toys and treats. A boy or girl who looked like one back home might find an extra coin pressed into his or her hand to buy a special toy.

Or diggers might select families of needy children to be fitted with new boots and shoes or fancy dresses and expensive suits. Children who encountered diggers on the street often arrived home with all the lollies, fancy ribbons, and tiny treasures they could carry. And packages filled with lovely lockets and other fancy delights— the gifts of secret admirers—would arrive on the doorstep of pretty young ladies.

In the goldfield camps, miners would slip gold nuggets into the plum pudding they shared, in place of traditional coins. The delight in going "prospecting" with a fork and spoon left many miners, ladies, and children with a full and satisfied feeling at the end of the Christmas meal.

Australia's Christmases of long ago may have not been the merriest or most festive occasions this continent has ever experienced. But they built the foundation upon which today's celebrations have grown. And as time has passed, Australians have woven the customs of yesteryear with new traditions that will be passed on for generations to come.

This engraving shows Elizabeth Street in Melbourne during the 1860's. Many of the buildings that line the streets of downtown Melbourne sprang up in the wake of the gold rush of the 1800's.

An Outback
CHRISTMAS

The vast interior of Australia is the famous outback. It consists mainly of wide, open countryside. Scattered throughout are small towns. Between these towns are isolated homesteads linked by lonely roads. The outback population is spread out on sheep and cattle stations, some of which cover more than 1,000 square miles. These stations may be 100 miles or more from the nearest town.

The outback is a land of climatic contrasts. The northern half is a land of cyclones, monsoons, and tropical vegetation. The southern half is the exact opposite, with deserts, dust, and a lot of red rocks. From one Christmas to the next there is no telling what the weather may bring. In some years, the temperature has been known to top 110 °F, and the holidays have been overshadowed by droughts, raging bushfires, drenching downpours, and dangerous floods. But for other Christmases, the outback's weather has made it heaven on earth. No matter what the weather, however, the people here know how to celebrate the season.

Youngsters crowd around Santa Claus as he makes a stop in the outback on Christmas Day.

A squatter (rancher) and her daughter enjoy a horseback ride on a station (ranch) in the outback.

The weather in the outback at Christmastime is often all about excesses. In some years, long stretches of no rain leading up to Christmas leave the grassy plains easy prey for fast and furious bushfires. In fact, Christmas Day accounts from early settlers often report neighbors joining together to beat sparks from the bush. They would dig trenches in the unbearable heat in all-out battles to save any homes they could. Then they would scramble to take cover in the creek as fires swept across the plains. Reports from other years tell of the best present coming from on high: a drenching, saving rain arriving right on Christmas morning.

But then, rain also can be a problem. Just when friends and families everywhere are coming together to celebrate the season, the isolation of life on an outback station can be intensified as driving rains and floods cut off farmers and their families from the rest of the world for weeks at a time.

In the remembrance *Green Mountains*, written in 1940, Bernard O'Reilly describes one Christmas Eve when "there were three little ones with implicit faith in Santa Claus, and three ex-

A camel ride on Cable Beach in Broome is one way to enjoy Christmas Day in Western Australia.

mas is Broome, in Western Australia's far north. For years, the citizens of Broome had depended on pearling for their livelihood. In the early 1900's, 300 to 400 sailing boats employing 3,000 men provided most of the world's mother-of-pearl shell. Many of the pearlers were Japanese, Malaysians, and Filipinos, and the town is still multiracial. Today Broome is a popular vacation spot all the year around.

Christmas Day in Broome is likely to be near 90 °F and 100 percent humidity. Still, the hotels and restaurants are air-conditioned, so many indulge in a full old-fashioned Christmas feast of hot turkey and all the trimmings. Others opt for a Christmas tradition started long ago—a camel ride on local Cable Beach, a very long and wide stretch of perfect Western Australian sand.

OUTBACK CHRISTMASES PAST

In anticipation of Christmas Day, outback families of yesteryear would scrub their homes, whitewash the walls, or put up new wallpaper, even if in hard times it was only new newspaper.

Next they would drape green boughs of gum trees and Australian "Christmas bush," with its lush red flowers, over pictures, doorways, and mantles. They also might hang native Australian mistletoe from the center of the ceiling—not so much to land kisses for shy ranchhands as to divert flies from the holiday table below.

Outside, they would strap great armfuls of greenery to every post of the veranda (a wide porch).

The outback holiday celebration centered on a lavish traditional Christmas dinner. Exactly how lavish and how traditional varied according to circumstance—and to what game was brought home on Christmas Eve. The spirit of the celebration, however, never wavered. Turkey and trimmings in the outback might have changed to kangaroo, lamb, parrot, cockatoo, pigeon, or duck. Side dishes consisted of the exotic fruits and vegetables that grew from the land. Wassail and hot tea were quickly dropped for cool drinks. Dessert, however, did not change—plum pudding was always a must. Procuring the ingredients and getting the "plum-duff" made were challenges often recorded in the journals of early Australian settlers, as in this account from Francis Augustus Hare, written in 1895:

Kabobs skewered with a variety of meats and vegetables are popular fare in the outback.

> "The first thing, we set to work to make our Christmas dinner—I remember it as though it were yesterday. I bought the materials for a plum pudding; for a dozen of eggs I gave £1*. I forget the prices of the raisins, etc., but I shall never forget the pudding! We boiled it for 24 hours! It took us a week to digest. It was as hard as a cannonball! It lasted a long time and was something to remember!"
>
> * equal to approximately $1.60

At lonely campfires in the bush, there was hardly a man who didn't try his own version of "billy can plum pudding." The ever-ready tin can that served in camp as a kettle for making hot tea would be put to use in creating some semblance of the familiar Christmas comfort.

Getting together for the holidays was the first priority at Christmas and the greatest challenge for citizens of the outback. Sons of squatters (ranchers) might be working far and wide as shearers, drovers, fencers, station hands, prospectors, stockmen, and bush roustabouts. Accounts of Christmases past tell the thrill of seeing Bob or Jim "cantering up the track with a valise strapped in front of him and a smoke-cloud trailing behind, while the old folks and the little ones are watching with glad faces from the veranda."

Around the Christmas table and well into the night, reunited brothers had plenty to report. Outback families have always been fond of storytelling, and "yarning" is still a central part of the Christmas celebration. With family members scattered across this vast land, stories have always been plentiful and audiences eager to hear every word.

When friends arrived from the farms nearby, the music and dancing would start. To the sound of a lone violin, lively jigs and stomps could rattle the crockery and quickly fill a room with Christmas cheer.

While the winds and the rains play their tricks, cards and letters from distant relations are delayed, and Christmas presents ordered through the mail may get lost, adverse weather cannot stop Christmas from coming to the outback. It is greeted with a hearty welcome at every isolated outpost. And this has been the case from Christmases past to Christmases present. Families of the outback still enjoy getting together with friends and families for this holy holiday. There is nothing quite like retiring to the veranda, a wide porch that surrounds many of the old farmhouses of the outback, after a satisfying Christmas dinner. Here farm families gather in the shade, catch what breeze is blowing, chat, and relax as they look out over their farms and the countryside.

Santa spreads some Christmas cheer to station hands in the outback.

Boxing Day: A Sporting
GOOD TIME

And, oh, how pleased his lordship was
    and how he smiled to say,
"That's good, my boy. Come, tell me now;
    and what is Christmas Day?"
The ready answer bared a fact
    no bishop ever knew—
"It's the day before the races
    out at Tangmalangaloo."

from *Tangmalangaloo* by P.J. Hartigan

There is none of that day-after-Christmas
let-down feeling in Australia. Boxing Day
immediately follows Christmas, bringing
enough sporting fun to satisfy every person
in this sports-loving land.

The Sydney skyline provides the backdrop for the Sydney-to-Hobart Yacht Race held on Boxing Day.

Boxing Day is filled with sporting events, including the Boxing Day cricket test match held in Melbourne. Cricket is an English game played with a ball and a bat with a flat hitting surface.

Boxing Day originated in Great Britain as a special observance on the day after Christmas for servants and shopkeepers who had been required to work while others celebrated. According to some versions of the custom's origin, the "boxes" of Boxing Day were those filled with clothing and other personal items given to servants as fine gentlemen's and ladies' closets were cleaned to make way for new Christmas finery. In another version, the boxes were those held out by the serving class to receive coins in thanks for service on this special day.

In Australia today, Boxing Day is a major national holiday and, given the sporting nature of the celebration, *boxing* literally stands for boxing here—or maybe sailing, football, swimming, volleyball, biking, or cricket.

The foremost sporting event of Boxing Day in Australia is the world-class Sydney-to-Hobart yacht race. This blue-water classic mixes little 30-foot upstarts with multi-million-dollar maxi-yachts in a 630-nautical-mile race down the east coast of Australia and across the treacherous Tasman Sea to Hobart, the capital of Tasmania.

At 1:00 p.m. on December 26, more than 300,000 people line the shore at Sydney Harbour with binoculars and champagne, ready to toast the racers off when the starter gun sounds on tiny Shark Island. The race, which first took place in 1945 with only 9 yachts, now regularly boasts a fleet of more than 100 boats from all over Australia, Great Britain, Japan, New Zealand, and the United States.

One day later, a similar scene occurs farther down the coast as 140 yachts set off in a second race to the same finish, the Melbourne-to-Hobart Yacht Race. Mixing in with the competitors from the Sydney race, they battle the dangerous waters of the Tasman Sea and Bass Strait. Their goal: a safe arrival at Constitution Dock in Hobart and a traditional scallop pie.

Waiting at the end of both races is a reward fitting the challenge: the Hobart Summer Festival. Everywhere along the waterfront in Tasmania's capital city, the festival is in high gear all during the Christmas holiday season.

At the heart of the celebration during the week between Christmas and New Year's Day is "A Taste of Tasmania." Here, more than 65 booths offer prized Tasmanian foods and wines. There are scallops, oysters, charcoal-grilled quail, salmon, and more—all prepared by gourmet chefs—plus highly rated local cheeses and champagne.

The racers and thousands of other party-loving people are sure to be in Hobart for the city's all-out New Year's Eve bash. The celebration offers plenty of food, fun, fireworks, and the charm of an Australian seaside summer night.

ALL-AROUND FUN

The roster for Boxing Day sporting events offers something for everyone. A variety of competitions are held all around Australia on this day.

In Melbourne, the Melbourne Cricket Ground stadium is packed for the Boxing Day cricket test match. As many as 90,000 spectators come on this day to watch two teams take to the field to compete in Australia's number-one summer sport. A test match is a bit different from a regular match in that the game is much more formal—the players dress in white— and it lasts from 4 to 5 days.

On the other side of the country, tennis greats from around the world gather at the Burswood Casino for the annual battle for the Hopman Cup.

What's the Word?

footy . . . . Australian-rules football

g'day . . . . good day

she'll be right . . . . . everything will be all right

shoot through . . . . . leave in a hurry

Santa Claus takes part in some pretty silly stunts during his visit to Australia. Here he is seen freefalling over the vast expanse of the outback.

In Corowa, on the southern border of New South Wales, there's the National Skydiving Championships. Skydivers make more than 1,000 jumps as they compete in formation, freestyle, and accuracy events.

Boxing Day is the date for the annual Highland Heavy Games in Daylesford, Victoria. Dressed in Scottish kilts and finery, competitors throw the shot put, hurl the hammer, and toss end over end a long, heavy wooden pole called a caber. An all-around celebration of Scottish tradition, the games also include competitions for bands, pipers, drummers, and highland dancers.

The Golden Spurs Rodeo on Boxing Day in Mytleford, Victoria, draws riders from across Australia to participate in various competitions.

Boxing Day also is the date for the triennial Australian Deaf Games. Athletes ages 14 to 78 compete in sporting events of every kind, from basketball and soccer to darts, golf, tennis, and swimming.

And there is plenty going on for those who would rather do than watch when it comes to Boxing Day sports. Everywhere families gather for cricket, tennis, or volleyball matches. Or perhaps they take part in "Aussie Rules" football, their very own version of the game.

Australia has some of the world's finest surfing beaches, and they are in full use on this national holiday. And wintertime skiing resorts are at capacity during the summer Christmas holidays as people head to the hills to hike, camp, fish, and explore.

THE SILLY SEASON

Maybe it's because people call them Antipodeans—the exact opposite of the usual; contrary. Maybe it comes from living "down under." Maybe it's because it's 100 °F on Christmas Day in Australia while Jack Frost is nipping at noses elsewhere. Maybe it's just because Christmas falls at the beginning of summer—the Silly Season in Australia.

Whatever the reason, Australians, who love turning serious subjects on their heads and who would rather enjoy a good laugh than complain in adversity, have always included lots of good, silly fun in their Christmas cheer.

At Thredbo, a popular resort in Australia's ski country, December 27 is the date for the annual wacky ski races. The snow's pretty much of a no-show, but the skiers are there—in shorts and bikinis—to attempt a run down whatever snowdrift might be there at the mountaintop. The skiing leaves much to be desired, but the barbecue and live entertainment are great. And all is for a good cause—the Disabled Skiers Association.

Living in remote isolation all year long, residents of the outback towns of Mataranka, Manyaluluk, Borroloola, and beyond team up to celebrate in style around Christmas in neighboring

Tennis is a popular sport in Australia. The Australian Open, held in January, is one of four Grand Slam events in the world and is held in Melbourne.

Katherine. For one grand night, Katherine's main road, Stuart Highway, is closed to traffic and open for fun. With great food, dancing, singing, bands, clowns, and more, these hardy Australians fill the great southern sky with Christmas cheer.

In Derby, a small town some 1,550 miles northeast of Perth, a zany sports carnival has been part of the Christmastime celebration for a quarter of a century. On Boxing Day, the Derbians, and those adventurous enough to join their silliness, compete in the Cockroach Crawl, Crab Flaps, Frog Flying, Cackleberry Chuckle, Lemon Drop Seed Spit, and more. Some lucky lady will even be crowned Cockroach Queen before the day is over.

The Moyston Boxing Day Sports competition near Ararat in western Victoria is all about bush skills. From rabbit skinning to tractor pulling to woodchopping to the soft-drink slurp, the contest puts plenty of serious and silly abilities to the test.

From Perth to Sydney and from Adelaide to the outback, all of Australia is abuzz with Christmas activity during the holiday season. And the variety of festivities offered at this time of year is as diverse as the people who live in this vast, open continent.

Junior surfers are on their marks and ready to compete in Palm Cove, Queensland.

Australian CRAFTS

MATERIALS*

~ scissors
~ colorful wrapping paper or tissue paper
~ one small cardboard tube
~ tape
~ paper
~ pen
~ small wrapped candies
~ confetti
~ two 8-inch lengths of ribbon

* Makes one cracker.

CHRISTMAS CRACKER

WHAT TO DO

1. Cut a piece of wrapping paper or tissue paper twice as long as the cardboard tube and wide enough to wrap around it with about 2 inches of overlap.

2. On a small piece of paper, write down a joke, Christmas wish, or fortune. Fold up the paper so it will fit inside the cardboard tube.

3. Put tape over one end of the cardboard tube to seal it. In the other end, insert candies, confetti, and the piece of paper with your message.

4. Place the tube in the center of the wrapping paper or tissue paper and wrap up the tube, being careful not to spill the contents. Tape the seam.

5. Tie one of the lengths of ribbon around the paper at one end of the tube and make a bow. If desired, curl the ribbon with the scissors. Repeat with the other end.

6. Make more Christmas crackers to share with friends or relatives, especially at a holiday meal. To open the crackers, untie the ribbons and unwrap the tubes.

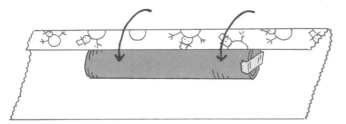

KOOKABURRA BIRD IN A EUCALYPTUS WREATH

Note: Children under the age of 10 should not use the glue gun alone. Young children will also need adult supervision with the pins.

MATERIALS

- one 4-oz. package green eucalyptus branches*
- one 12-inch twig wreath
- two 2⅜" x 1⅞" Styrofoam™ eggs
- scissors
- one white pipe cleaner
- one black pipe cleaner
- dark brown, light brown, and white feathers
- glue gun with glue sticks
- straight pins
- two brown pipe cleaners

* Try to select flexible, not dried-out, branches.

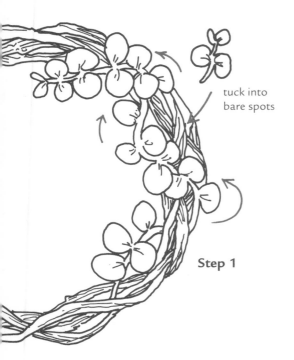

tuck into bare spots

Step 1

WHAT TO DO

1. To make the wreath, break the smaller eucalyptus branches off the longer ones. Wrap the longer branches around the perimeter of the twig wreath, weaving the ends of the branches into the twigs. Working your way toward the center, cover as much of the twig wreath as desired, using the smaller eucalyptus branches to fill in the bare spots.

2. To make the kookaburra bird, cut one of the Styrofoam™ eggs in half as shown.

3. Cut a 2-inch length of white pipe cleaner and stick it halfway into the top side of the narrow end of the other Styrofoam™ egg. Stick the narrow end of the cut Styrofoam™ egg (from Step 2) onto the other end of the pipe cleaner.

4. For the bird's eyes, cut two ½-inch lengths of black pipe cleaner. Stick these all the way into the bird's head so that just the ends can be seen.

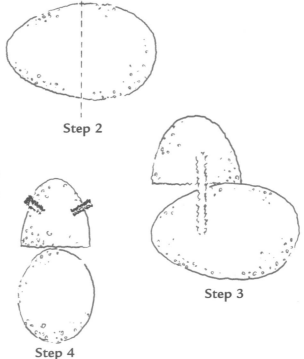

Step 2

Step 3

Step 4

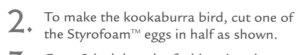

5. Cover the bird's head with three white feathers by first sticking the pointed ends of the feathers into the Styrofoam™ at the sides and back of the bird's head. Next, apply hot glue to the feathers and then hold them against the Styrofoam™. To secure them in place, affix the feathers with straight pins, making sure the pins go through the "spines" of the feathers. Allow the glue to dry for about an hour. If desired, remove the pins once the glue dries.

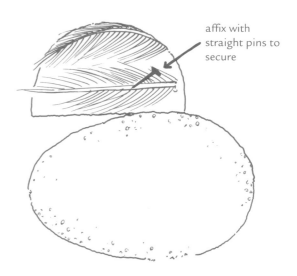

affix with straight pins to secure

6. Cover the body of the bird with dark brown, light brown, and white feathers. Stick the pointed ends into the Styrofoam™ around the entire body, allowing the feathers to stick up. Add as many feathers as desired.

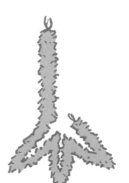

7. For the bird's feet, cut two 3- to 4-inch lengths of brown pipe cleaner. Bend each one at one end to form three toes, leaving at least 1 inch of pipe cleaner for the legs. Stick the legs into the Styrofoam™ on the underside of the bird.

8. For the bird's beak, cut a 3-inch length of brown pipe cleaner. Bend the pipe cleaner into the shape of a long bird's beak. Stick the ends into the Styrofoam™ head, securing it in place.

9. Hang the eucalyptus wreath on a nail from one of the twigs on the backside of the wreath. Attach the kookaburra bird to the wreath by wrapping the bird's feet around any branch on the wreath.

GLITTER ORNAMENT

Note: This ornament will take a few days to dry.

Be sure to do this project well in advance of using it.

MATERIALS

~ pen

~ waxed paper

~ glue

~ glitter of various colors, such as green, red, gold, and silver

~ needle and thread

WHAT TO DO

1. With the pen, carefully draw or trace a Christmas shape—such as the candle in a candle holder, candy cane, star, and Christmas tree shown here—on the waxed paper. The ink from the pen will not appear, but the pen will etch your drawing onto the waxed paper.

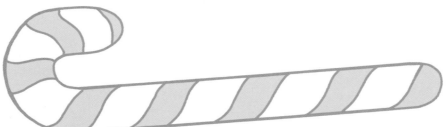

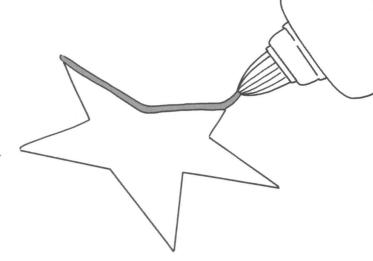

2. Cover the area inside the outline with a thin layer of glue. Immediately sprinkle glitter on top of the glue, being sure to cover all the glue. Use different colors of glitter for the different parts of the picture. Allow the glue to dry completely; this could take a day or two.

3. Once the glue is dry, slowly and carefully peel the ornament off the wax paper.

4. Turn the ornament glitter side down and cover the exposed dry glue with another thin layer of glue. Again, sprinkle glitter all over the glue, using the same color pattern as on the first side. Allow the glue to dry for a day or two.

5. Once the ornament is dry, make a hanger for it by threading a needle and thread through the top of the ornament. Tie a loop and cut.

BAY LEAF TREE CENTERPIECE

Note: Young children will need adult supervision with the pins.

MATERIALS

~ one 8- to 10-inch green Styrofoam™ cone
~ two 12-oz jars bay leaves
~ straight pins
~ sequins and beads
~ gold star sticker

WHAT TO DO

1. Beginning at the bottom of the cone, carefully pin the bay leaves to the cone in an overlapping pattern, pointed end facing downward. Cover the entire cone with leaves.

2. Decorate the tree by pinning sequins and small beads wherever you wish.

3. Affix the star sticker to the top of the tree.

Australian CAROLS

CHRISTMAS IN AUSTRALIA

Words and Music by Lorna C. Parker

CHORUS

Christ - mas in Aust - ra - lia means man - y things to man - y pe - o - ple,

alto glockenspiel

Christ - mas in Aust - ra - lia means man - y things to me.

VERSE

Mem - or - ies of Yule-tide, mid - win - ter, the Yule log,

Snow - men on the hill-top, and cand-les on the tree.

Angels in the Heavens
The Wise Men, the Shepherds
Jesus in the stable
Asleep on Mary's knee.

Happy times with families,
The turkey, the pudding,
Jingle Bells and Santa,
And presents on the tree.

Golden sands on beaches
The surfboards, the sailboats,
Lying in the sunshine
And swimming in the sea.

O LITTLE BABE OF BETHLEHEM

Music by Lewis H. Redner, 1868-1908 [WE]
Words by Mother Francis Frewin, IBVM

O lit-tle Babe of Beth-le-hem! The Sou-thern_ Cross shines down, As

once a Star shone glor-i-ous a-bove an___ east-ern town.

The hearts of Bethlehem are cold,
The streets are hushed with snow,
The doors are barred, there is no room,
Dear Lord, where wilt Thou go?

O come, sweet Jesus, come to us!
Australia's sun is warm,
And here are loving hearts enough
To shield Thee from the storm.

Come! we will give Thee all we have,
Each bird and flower and tree,
The breeze that stirs the silver gums,
The music of the sea.

And sweet wild clématis starry-eyed,
With delicate ferns we'll bring;
Our wattle trees shall shower their gold
In tribute to our King.

We'll watch, when evening sounds begin,
And dreaming flowers nod,
Thy Mother fold Thee in her arms,
Thou little Lamb of God.

Bell-birds shall ring their silver peal
From gullies green and deep,
And mingle with the magpies' note
To call Thee from Thy sleep.

O little Babe of Bethlehem
Australia loves Thee well,
Come to our hearts this Christmastide,
And there forever dwell.

Australian
RECIPES

AUSTRALIAN MEAT PIE

1½ lbs. boneless sirloin
   steak (uncooked),
   minced
2 tsp. beef bouillon
   granules

1½ cups water
salt and pepper to taste
¼ tsp. nutmeg
2 tbsp. cornstarch
¼ cup water

1 tsp. soy sauce
two 9-inch refrigerated
   pie dough rounds
1 egg yolk
1 tsp. water

For the filling, brown the steak in a large skillet. Remove from heat and drain off
excess fat. Return meat to medium-high heat; add bouillon, 1½ cups of water,
salt, pepper, and nutmeg. Stir until mixture comes to a boil. Reduce heat, cover,
and simmer gently for 20 minutes, then remove from heat.

In a small bowl, combine cornstarch and ¼ cup water, stirring until mixture is
smooth. Add cornstarch mixture to the meat and stir until well combined. Return
meat to heat; stirring until thickened. Add soy sauce; mix well. Simmer, uncov-
ered, 5 to 10 minutes. Remove mixture from heat and allow to cool completely.

Meanwhile, line a 9-inch pie plate with one of the refrigerated pie dough rounds.
Fill with cooled meat filling. Top with the other pie dough round by wetting edges
of base pastry and gently pressing top into place. Trim around the edge with a
knife as needed.

Combine egg yolk and remaining water. Brush the top of the pastry with this mixture. Bake according to the pie dough package directions.

Makes 8 servings

SUNSHINE SALAD

6 cups cooked elbow
   macaroni
4 cups blanched green
   beans, cut in half

2 red peppers, cut into
   fine strips
2 cups celery, finely
   chopped

2 cups green onions,
   chopped
½ cup mayonnaise
8 large lettuce leaves

Combine all ingredients except lettuce leaves in a large salad bowl and
toss thoroughly. Chill until ready to serve. Serve on lettuce leaves.

Makes 8 servings

AUSTRALIAN SHRIMP ON THE BARBIE

1 stick butter, melted
3 garlic cloves, crushed
¼ cup olive oil
1 tbsp. minced fresh parsley
1 tbsp. minced fresh thyme
1 tbsp. minced fresh cilantro
1 tbsp. finely minced green onion

salt, to taste
freshly ground pepper, to taste
1½ lb. medium or large shrimp, unpeeled
3 tbsp. fresh lemon juice
spinach leaves
8 lemon slices

In a large mixing bowl, combine melted butter, garlic, olive oil, parsley, thyme, cilantro, green onions, salt, and pepper; stir to mix thoroughly. Add shrimp, mixing so as to evenly coat each piece. Marinate shrimp at room temperature for 1 hour or in the refrigerator for 5 hours, stirring occasionally.

Prepare traditional barbecue grill with medium-hot coals or a gas barbecue grill to medium heat. Thread shrimp onto 8 skewers. Grill until just opaque, about 2 minutes per side. Line a serving platter with spinach leaves. Arrange skewers on platter. Sprinkle fresh lemon juice over shrimp. Garnish with lemon slices and serve.

Makes 8 servings

KANGAROO AND MUSHROOMS WITH RED WINE

Kangaroo is a very rich meat that is low in cholesterol.
Ask your local (specialty) meat distributor to order it for you.

½ cup (1 stick) butter
2 lbs. loin fillet of kangaroo
1 cup sliced mushrooms
1 cup red wine

Melt the butter in a large iron frying pan. Brown kangaroo steak on both sides, then quickly slice into pieces about ¾-inch thick. Add mushrooms. Brown the slices on both sides until the steak is nearly cooked, being careful not to cook it too well done. (Meat should be still a little pink inside.) Pour in the red wine and continue cooking for a few more minutes. Serve on individual serving dishes, pouring a bit of the liquid over each serving.

Makes 6 to 8 servings

CRABMEAT AND SPINACH ROULADE

2 tbsp. butter
3 tbsp. flour
1 cup milk
3 eggs, separated
1 small can crabmeat

¼ lb. spinach, cooked and well-drained
½ cup ricotta cheese
pepper to taste

Melt butter in a small saucepan; stir in flour. Gradually add milk, stirring constantly, while bringing to a boil. Remove from heat and beat in egg yolks. Allow mixture to cool completely.

In a medium mixing bowl, beat egg whites until stiff. Gently fold in cooled egg-yolk mixture. Pour into a greased and floured jellyroll pan lined with waxed paper, and bake for 30 minutes at 325 °F.

Place a clean dish towel on a wire rack and turn roulade out onto the towel. Slowly remove the waxed paper. Quickly but gently roll up the roulade. Allow to cool.

Meanwhile, prepare the filling. Combine the crabmeat, spinach, ricotta cheese, and pepper. Once cooled, unroll the roulade and spread with filling. Roll up the roulade again, cut into 8 slices, and serve.

Makes 8 servings

GRILLED GRAPEFRUIT

4 large grapefruit
1 tbsp. butter, melted
2 tbsp. brown sugar
1 tsp. allspice
4 maraschino cherries, cut in half

Cut grapefruit in half, cut away and discard center core and remove all seeds. Using a grapefruit spoon or small knife, loosen pulp into segments. In a small bowl, combine melted butter, brown sugar, and allspice. Spread this mixture on top of each grapefruit. Place on grill and cook 4 minutes or until lightly browned. You can also cook the grapefruit in the microwave on high power for 30 seconds. Garnish with halved cherries.

Makes 8 servings

STUFFED ACORN SQUASH

1 cup lentils, uncooked	2 bay leaves	1½ cups cottage cheese
3 cups water	8 medium acorn squash	1 cup breadcrumbs
1 cup brown rice, uncooked	1 cup mushrooms, sliced	2 tbsp. grated Parmesan cheese
3 cups chicken broth	2 stalks celery, chopped	
	4 tbsp. dill	2 tsp. paprika

Soak lentils in 3 cups water for 1 hour. Drain, rinse, and drain again. In a large saucepan, combine lentils, rice, chicken broth, and bay leaves over medium-high heat. Bring mixture to a boil, cover, reduce heat, and simmer for 30 to 35 minutes, until liquid is absorbed. Remove bay leaves.

While lentils are cooking, pierce the squash in several places with a fork. Bake directly on the oven rack at 350 °F for 25 minutes. (Line the bottom of the oven with aluminum foil to catch drippings.) Remove squash from oven, cut off stem ends and top inch, and scoop out the seeds. Slice half an inch off bottom of each squash. Place squash upright in a large, deep, well-greased baking pan.

In a medium bowl, combine lentil mixture, mushrooms, celery, dill, and cottage cheese. Divide this mixture among the squash, filling them almost to the top. In a small bowl, combine breadcrumbs, Parmesan cheese, and paprika. Sprinkle this mixture on top of squash. Bake at 350 °F for 25 minutes.

Makes 8 servings

DAMPER (BREAD)

2 ½ cups bread flour
1 tsp. salt
1 tsp. butter
1 tsp. sugar
1 cup milk
jam, butter, or syrup (optional)

Preheat oven to 350 °F. Using a fork, mix together the flour, salt, butter, and sugar. Add the milk and mix well. Turn dough onto a lightly floured surface and knead for about 5 minutes. Shape the dough into a ball and then flatten it out. Place on a well-greased and floured baking sheet. Bake for 30 minutes or until golden on top.

Slice the bread into thick slices while still hot. Serve warm with jam, butter, and/or syrup.

Makes 1 damper

CHEESE AND SAGE DAMPER

2 cups bread flour
¾ cup cheddar cheese,
   grated
½ tsp. paprika
¼ tsp. pepper
1 tsp. dried sage

¼ cup (½ stick) butter or
   margarine, softened
1 cup evaporated skim milk
3 tsp. milk
2 tsp. Parmesan cheese,
   grated
2 tsp. poppy seeds

Preheat oven to 350 °F. In a large mixing bowl, combine flour, cheddar cheese, paprika, pepper, and sage. Add butter, or margarine, and mix with a fork until mixture is crumbly. Add evaporated milk and mix to form a soft dough. Turn dough out onto a lightly floured surface. Knead dough and shape into an 8-inch round. Using a sharp knife, cut 8 wedges almost through the dough. Brush the top of the dough with milk and sprinkle with Parmesan cheese and poppy seeds. Bake for 25 to 30 minutes. When slightly cooled, cut through wedges and serve.

Makes 1 damper

SPICED PEARS

2 cups water
2 cups red wine
¼ cup lemon juice
2 cups sugar
2 sticks cinnamon
2 tsp. whole allspice
8 firm pears, peeled with stems still attached
whipped cream

Combine water, red wine, lemon juice, sugar, and spices in a medium saucepan; bring to a boil. Reduce heat and simmer gently for 5 minutes. Place the pears in an ovenproof dish and pour the syrup over them. Bake at 300 °F for 20 to 25 minutes, until pears are tender.

To serve, pour a small amount of the syrup in the bottom of each serving dish. Place one pear in each dish. Serve with whipped cream.

Makes 8 servings

PAVLOVA

4 egg whites
pinch of salt
1 cup sugar
½ tsp. vanilla
¾ tsp. vinegar

½ pint heavy cream
sliced kiwi fruit, strawberries,
    bananas, passion fruit pulp,
    or other fresh or well-
    drained canned fruit

Preheat oven to 250 °F. Line a baking sheet with waxed paper. Using a bowl or plate, trace a 7-inch circle onto the paper.

In a medium bowl, beat the egg whites and salt until soft peaks form. Add ⅓ cup of the sugar and beat until the sugar is dissolved and the mixture is very thick. Add the rest of the sugar, 1 tablespoon at a time, beating well after each addition. When the sugar is dissolved and the mixture is very stiff, add the vanilla and vinegar. Beat to combine the ingredients. The mixture will be thick and glossy, like a meringue.

Spoon the meringue mixture into the circle marked on the waxed paper. Using the back of a spoon, spread out the meringue evenly within the circle, building up the sides. Bake for 1½ hours or until firm to the touch. Turn off the oven and cool the "pav" in the oven, leaving the door open slightly.

Using an electric mixer, whip the heavy cream in a chilled bowl until stiff. Wash and slice the fruit, using as many different kinds as you like. If using passion fruit, cut it in half and scoop out the pulp.

To serve, spread the whipped cream over the top of the cooled meringue. Evenly arrange the fruit on top of the cream. Cut into wedges and serve immediately.

Makes 8 servings

PUMPKIN SCONES

¼ cup (½ stick) butter
1 cup sugar
2 eggs

one 16-oz. can pumpkin
4 cups bread flour
dash of salt

Preheat oven to 425 °F. With an electric mixer, cream together the butter and sugar until light and fluffy. Add eggs and beat well. Gently fold in canned pumpkin, flour, and salt. Gently knead the dough until soft. Pinch off 1-inch pieces, shape into small squares, and place on a well-greased baking sheet. Bake until well risen and golden, about 15 minutes. Serve hot with butter.

Makes 8 to 12 servings